Forever 36

FOREVER 36

THE JOURNEY THROUGH GRIEF AFTER THE SUICIDE OF A FAMILY MEMBER

KELI HOFFMANN

FOREVER 36 The Journey through Grief after the Suicide of a Family Member
Copyright © 2021 by KELI HOFFMANN

All rights reserved. No part of this publication may be reproduced, distributed, or transmitted in any form or by any means, including photocopying, recording, or other electronic or mechanical methods, without the prior written permission of the author, except in the case of brief quotations embodied in critical reviews and certain other noncommercial uses permitted by copyright law.

Disclaimer:

The author strives to be as accurate and complete as possible in the creation of this book, notwithstanding the fact that the author does not warrant or represent at any time that the contents within are accurate due to the rapidly changing nature of the Internet.

While all attempts have been made to verify information provided in this publication, the Author and the Publisher assume no responsibility and are not liable for errors, omissions, or contrary interpretation of the subject matter herein. The Author and Publisher hereby disclaim any liability, loss or damage incurred as a result of the application and utilization, whether directly or indirectly, of any information, suggestion, advice, or procedure in this book. Any perceived slights of specific persons, peoples, or organizations are unintentional.

In practical advice books, like anything else in life, there are no guarantees of income made. Readers are cautioned to rely on their own judgment about their individual circumstances to act accordingly. Readers are responsible for their own actions, choices, and results. This book is not intended for use as a source of legal, business, accounting or financial advice. All readers are advised to seek the services of competent professionals in legal, business, accounting, and finance field.

Printed in the United States of America

ISBN: 978-1-948382-14-4 paperback
JMP2021.2

For my parents, who lost a son
but gained an angel.

And for Doug. I will carry your memory
with me until we meet again.

Contents

Prologue 1

The Beginning 5

Grief 9

Letters to Heaven 15

Final Goodbye 19

Back to Reality 25

Lingering Questions 31

Support 45

Hope 59

Turning Point 67

Faith Crisis	77
Unhappy Birthdays	83
Searching for Purpose	95
Letting Go	105
Honoring Their Memory	113
Author's Biography	119

Prologue

I arrived home on January 26, 2020, at approximately 5:10 p.m. I was in a great mood. I had discovered a leaky pipe in my wall about two weeks earlier and had been dealing with plumbers and a mold remediation company ever since. After several days of loud dehumidifiers running constantly, the mold was finally gone, the plumbing was fixed, and my house was quiet at last. I had just finished a long twelve-hour shift as a deputy sheriff at a jail and was only one more shift away from what I expected to be my first relaxing weekend of the new year.

I had stepped in something questionable at work, so as soon as I set foot on my front porch, I bent down to take my shoes off. I was so focused that it took me a moment to recognize what I was seeing. My dog, Zoey, was standing on the other side of the screen door, her tail wagging in excitement. Ordinarily this would have been a welcome sight. The problem was, I hadn't unlocked or opened my front door yet. Zoey and I lived alone, so unless she had managed to open the door herself, someone else was in my house.

My dad suddenly appeared behind Zoey, which provided momentary relief. The relief quickly turned into confusion and then irritation. After a long day at work, I was looking forward to a quiet night and early bedtime. My first assumption was that my dad was there checking out the work that had been done in my house. Although it would have been uncharacteristic of him to drop by without calling first, I could think of no other explanation. As I was trying to come up with a nice way to convey my exhaustion without hurting his feelings, my dad said the three words that would change my life forever: "Doug killed himself."

This is the story of my personal journey through grief in the months following my brother's suicide. Some names have been changed to protect their privacy. It's my sincere hope that my story will encourage others who are struggling in the aftermath of their loved ones' suicides.

If you're currently feeling suicidal, please reach out to the National Suicide Prevention Lifeline at 1-800-273-TALK (8255).

The Beginning

Doug was my big brother and only sibling. He was thirty-six, and I was thirty-four. Neither of us was married, nor did we have children. We lived approximately a hundred miles from each other in northeastern Colorado.

Doug and I were very close as we grew up. I wanted to be just like him, and I followed him around constantly. We built snow forts and skied together during the winter, and we played with squirt guns and went swimming in the summer. We frequently rode our bikes to a nearby gas station to buy candy cigarettes. After Doug got his driver's license, he would drive me to school and to my job at a dry cleaner, blaring music by the Bloodhound Gang and Weezer so loud the car would shake. He would let me shift gears from the passenger seat in an effort to teach me how to drive a manual transmission. He even attempted to teach his klutzy sister how to snowboard, despite both of us knowing I would spend far more time on my rear end than on my feet. I'm sure I bugged him more than I'll ever know, but he never complained. He was kind and patient, and had a wonderful sense of humor. Doug was the absolute biggest part of my childhood, and I was so grateful to have him. I never wanted to be an only child, and I never imagined I would be.

If I'm honest with myself, I have to acknowledge that Doug had been unhappy for the better part of twenty years. Things began going downhill in his teens, when he traded the candy cigarettes for real cigarettes and started hanging out with the "bad crowd" in high school. We did stay fairly close until our midtwenties, but our paths had gone in opposite directions. Sadly, we grew apart during the last ten years of his life, but I always had hope that our relationship would improve one day.

Although things would momentarily start getting better for Doug, the crash would inevitably come, and he fell further each time. I can't say that his suicide was a complete surprise, but I never really thought he would end his life. And I certainly didn't think he would do so while our parents were still alive. At the time, I was naïve enough to believe people are thinking clearly and rationally when they make that final decision.

I have struggled with the idea of writing this book. On one hand, it could help others going through something similar. I searched for books in the aftermath of my brother's suicide, only to come away disappointed. Most aren't written from a sibling's perspective; we're, unfortunately, the forgotten survivors. There have been several books written on the topic of suicide, but most focus on the author's life and the events leading up to the loved one's suicide. Hearing the specifics of one person's suicide doesn't help other suicide loss survivors heal. Telling our story is therapeutic for us, but it isn't particularly therapeutic for the audience. Readers want to know how to continue on after their heart has been shattered. They want to know that others have experienced a similar tragedy and survived. They want to know how to make it to the other side of grief.

Doug's story is his own, and I can't betray him by sharing it. I can, however, share my own story without going into the intimate details of his life and death. This is the compromise I have decided to make. After all, this book isn't intended for those contemplating suicide or those trying to prevent a loved one from taking their life: it's for those who have already lost a loved one to suicide.

Suicide prevention is extremely important, but I have neither the expertise nor experience to write on that topic. Instead, I'll write about the aftermath of suicide, something no one ever wants to experience but far too many have or will at some point. This isn't a book about loss; it's a book about surviving loss. It's meant to help fellow survivors pick up the pieces of their lives and put them back together as best they can. Loss changes us, but we get to determine whether those changes will be positive or negative. We bear no responsibility for our loved one's death, but we're responsible for our own healing.

Grief

Loss is a part of life, and grief is the price we pay for love. No two losses are the same, but there are five basic stages of grief outlined by psychiatrist Elisabeth Kübler-Ross that tend to be universal: denial, anger, bargaining, depression, and acceptance. However, grief isn't always linear, and there isn't a timeframe. It's entirely possible to make it through one stage of grief only to revisit it again days, weeks, months, or years later. It's also possible to skip a stage, as I did with bargaining.

The loss from suicide is more complicated because the stages of grief have added layers, and other emotions play a major role. Some of the more common emotions are confusion and guilt. My journey through grief has not been flawless, nor is it a perfect blueprint for everyone to follow, but I share it because it's comforting to know that you're not alone in dealing with this roller coaster of emotions.

There's a reason denial is listed first in the stages of grief. Denial is a defense mechanism used to protect us from something too emotionally painful to handle. When we lose someone we love, we can't believe they're truly gone and will never walk through our front door again. We want to believe that there has been some horrible mistake or that we're having a nightmare from which we will eventually awake.

With suicide, denial is twofold. First, we deny that our loved one is really dead. And then we often deny that they actually killed themselves. As a deputy, I have lost several friends and coworkers to suicide. One in particular bothered me, as I couldn't understand how David could voluntarily leave his young son. Many of us were convinced he was murdered, and that thought made me feel better. To this day, I'm not sure why I thought murder would be preferable to suicide, other than the stigma associated with the latter and the misconception that we're not enough for them to live. In reality, many people who take their lives do so because they believe their loved ones will be better off without them. In their eyes, their actions are selfless rather than selfish.

Anger is present after all losses, but it's especially complicated with suicide. In addition to being angry with God or the universe for taking our loved one from us, we have other targets. These include our loved one and anyone else we perceive to be a contributing factor, such as a significant other, a friend, a bully, an employer, or a coworker. We unwittingly become victims, and we want to place blame. Anger has its purpose; it's often easier to deal with than sadness. Anger gives us focus and can help us make it through necessary tasks. I was so angry at David that it enabled me to make it through his viewing and funeral, which I had to work as part of the honor guard. Sadness is far more debilitating than anger. Sadness tends to make us feel helpless, whereas anger motivates. In the short term, anger can provide a benefit, but it's necessary to move past this stage in order to heal.

Depression is perhaps the most dangerous stage for any loss, but this is especially true for suicide. The blunt truth is this: suicide often runs in families. In some cases, an underlying mental illness may be genetic. It's also possible that one suicide in the family may be seen as giving permission for others to follow suit. And, of course, people miss their loved ones so much they may see suicide as a way to be quickly reunited. The longer we're depressed and feel hopeless, the more at risk we become.

Any sudden death is bound to cause confusion, especially if there were no warning signs. One minute our loved ones are with us, and the next they're gone. We want to know why. The vast majority of suicides don't leave a note, but even if they do, questions will always remain. Intertwined with the confusion is guilt. What did we miss? What could we have done differently? Why wasn't our love enough for them to stay? If we had known that the last time we saw them would be the last time, what would we have said? Would it have made a difference? For this reason, and so many more, the guilt turns back into anger directed squarely at ourselves.

I have found myself lost in grief and depression, and I sympathize with those who are stuck there right now. Grief is meant to be a journey, not a destination. The following chapters will detail my long journey and how I managed to keep going when all I wanted to do was give up.

Letters to Heaven

After my parents went back home on January 26, I immediately called a trusted friend. Although she hadn't lost a sibling to suicide, she wasn't a stranger to loss, and I knew she would understand. When we hung up an hour later, I fell to my knees, wailing. I was never going to see my brother again, and the enormity was just beginning to set in. The initial shock lasted for about a week. I don't remember much, aside from eating and sleeping very little and crying a lot.

The first night I had the urge to write to Doug. I wanted to text—our favorite form of communication—but the police had his phone, and I didn't want them to see my private thoughts. So I grabbed some paper and a pen, and I wrote everything I was thinking. Everything I didn't get to say to him went into that letter. I would later discover that therapists often recommend doing this. To me, it was instinctual. I was his bratty little sister, and I wanted the last word!

My anger started coming out in that first letter, but I also reminisced about happy memories. They say that losing a sibling is like losing your past, present, and future. To an extent that's true of any loss, but because siblings are generally close in age, we grow up with them and expect to grow old with them. We have a shared history, and we assume they will always be a part of our future.

I had only planned on writing one letter to say goodbye, but letter writing became my routine. Every night I would write a letter and cry. I didn't miss one night for the first six weeks, and I felt horribly guilty after that first missed letter. But gradually, I got to the point where I would write two or three letters a week, and I have never missed a holiday. Basically, if I would have sent Doug a text or called while he was alive, I write him a letter now instead.

When I first started writing letters, I did it solely for me. Although Doug and I were raised Baptist and attended Sunday school and Awana every week, I had largely lost my faith as an adult. I stopped going to church and started questioning much of what I had been raised to believe. I continued my daily prayers to God—just in case—but the idea of life after death wasn't something with which I concerned myself. It didn't really matter . . . until it did.

During those early letters, I assumed Doug was just gone. I didn't want him to be, of course, but that was far better than him burning in hell, which is where I had been raised to believe people went after killing themselves. I'm not sure where this belief comes from, although it isn't uncommon in the Christian faith. As a chaplain pointed out to me shortly after Doug's death, nowhere in the Bible does it say suicide is a sin worthy of hell. In fact, the Bible is quite sympathetic to those who take their lives because it recognizes their suffering.

I put the idea of heaven and hell, and faith in general, on the back burner initially, but it would make a strong reappearance in the months ahead. But first, I had to get through my final goodbye and Doug's celebration of life.

Final Goodbye

Roughly ten years prior to Doug's death, our childhood friend died at the age of twenty-six. He was Catholic, so his funeral was an open-casket one. I had never been to this type of funeral before, and I was appalled. I thought it was awful that we had to remember him that way. In fact, seeing him lying in that casket is the only thing I remember from his service.

Approximately five years later, I was working David's viewing and funeral. I felt the same feeling of dread as I approached the casket. But this time, I felt something new wash over me as I looked down upon him: closure. I still remember David as he was: sweet, funny, and optimistic. Seeing him simply helped me pass through the first stage of grief: denial. I generally have to see in order to believe, and I could no longer deny what I had seen with my own eyes.

I'm not sure exactly what changed between the two funerals. I hadn't seen my childhood friend in many years and never knew him as an adult. Given the nature of our relationship, I would have been better served by not seeing him at the funeral. Conversely, I only knew David as an adult and saw him frequently. The memory of him lying in the casket is just one of many that I have of David, rather than the primary image seared into my brain.

When it came to Doug, I was adamant that I needed to see him. No one thought it was a good idea, and for some it undoubtedly wouldn't have been. It's a very individual choice, and what works for one person won't necessarily work for another. However, I knew that I would never be able to fully leave denial behind if I didn't see my brother one last time.

And so I did. I saw him, I touched his hand, and I told him I loved him. I have absolutely no regrets about seeing him, and I don't believe it caused me any unnecessary trauma. However, it's not my place to tell anyone else to do the same. There was a real benefit for me, but it's up to each person to decide if seeing their loved one would cause them more harm than good.

That was my way of saying goodbye, and neither my parents nor I wanted to have any kind of service. Doug was cremated on January 30, which was his half-birthday. Sadly, Doug didn't have many friends, and we weren't sure anyone would show up for a service. We were also not mentally equipped to plan any type of gathering at that time. However, one of Doug's friends contacted me and inquired about a service. Upon hearing there would be none, he grew angry. I finally gave in and reluctantly agreed to a celebration of life at a local park. His friend did everything regarding the invites, and all we had to do was provide food, pictures, and balloons.

We held the celebration of life on February 8, and I hated every second of it. I prefer to grieve privately, and I felt like I was on display. I found out later that Doug's friend had a falling out with him several months before his death, and I suddenly understood his insistence. He was dealing with his own feelings of guilt, and he wanted to do one last thing for his friend. The falling out wasn't his fault, but that's of little comfort when reconciliation is no longer possible. I understood his need for action to counter the helplessness he undoubtedly felt. I hope the celebration of life brought him some peace and closure.

I could relate to his friend because I had done something similar to try and ease my own guilt. Doug had taken in a stray cat a couple years earlier. Doug told us if anything happened to him, we should let the cat go. The cat had survived on his own once, and he would survive on his own again.

On my first visit to Doug's house, I noticed the cat hanging around the property. I let him into the house, and he scarfed down his food and drank some water. He was so friendly and sweet; it was hard to leave him outside in the cold. But I was simply unable to bring him home with me. My dog is incredibly antisocial, and it would have been a bloodbath. I'm not sure who would have won the fight, but I knew I didn't want to find out.

I went back to his house twice more over the next few days to check on the cat, and he was always on the property, waiting for Doug to come home. It broke my heart. I realized I couldn't leave him to fend for himself. So I worked tirelessly over the next couple days to find a home for him, and I finally did. One of Doug's high school friends happened to see my Facebook post, and he offered to give the cat a home. It was one last thing I could do for my brother. I couldn't save him, but I could save his cat. It helped ease a small fraction of the guilt I felt.

Back to Reality

The first week or two after a death is surreal. There's so much to do regarding funeral or celebration of life arrangements and settling the estate. Once all of the practicalities are out of the way, reality sets in. Even finding the motivation to get out of bed can be a struggle. Everyone is certainly different, but I knew for me, getting back to work and my routine was essential. I had reverted to a graveyard schedule in the aftermath of Doug's death, despite having switched to day shift in January, and my sleep schedule was suffering greatly.

On my first day back to work, I had a considerable amount of anxiety. I knew my entire team had been told what happened. Initially, I was upset about this, but in retrospect, it saved me a lot of heartache. Because everyone already knew, I didn't have to tell the story over and over. No one came up to me and asked how my "vacation" was, or made any other snide remarks that would have been innocent on their part but incredibly insensitive under the circumstances.

In order to return to work, I had to set some ground rules for myself. Most importantly, I didn't want to cry at work. Initially, I let myself cry before and after, but I quickly realized crying before work was a mistake. Showing up to work a blubbering mess was just as bad as breaking down at work. So I set aside time every night to cry.

Looking back, I see how utterly robotic that makes me sound. But I'm human, after all, and my plan didn't always go perfectly. There were days when I could feel the tears welling up. Someone would mention something innocent, like the word "brother," and I'd have to excuse myself.

On one occasion, an inmate was talking about an injury he sustained to his face after being hit by a baseball bat, and I teared up. I immediately flashed back to the time about thirty years ago when, in my five-year old wisdom, I brilliantly walked behind Doug as he was swinging a baseball bat. The bat connected with my left eyebrow, and I began gushing blood and screaming. Doug then began crying hysterically because he was scared he was going to get in trouble.

All it took was an innocent comment from an unsuspecting person to leave me reeling.

There's, unfortunately, no way to avoid this. Time helps, but those flashbacks will always appear when we least expect them. Setting aside time each day, or as often as you need, makes it less likely you'll break down at inopportune times.

Let's take a moment to talk about *triggers*. I would absolutely love it if everyone would refrain from saying "brother," "sister," and "sibling" in my presence. Those words feel like a knife to my heart. I would also appreciate it if they not talk about their own siblings within my earshot. But I also realize this isn't a practical request. We can't expect everyone to tiptoe around us. And frankly, I don't want that. I want people to feel comfortable talking to me without feeling like they have to censor everything they say. When people feel like they're walking on eggshells around us, they may ultimately decide to stop spending time around us.

I understand this may be controversial. It sounds like I'm saying that we must fake being okay in the presence of others so that we don't make them feel uncomfortable. But what I'm really saying is this: we can't control what others say and do, we can only control our reactions. We need to recognize our triggers and take the control away from these words and actions. Our triggers are our responsibility; we can't expect the world to cater to us. I'll never like the word "brother." The word "sibling" will always make me flinch. But I refuse to run and hide from these words. If a friend or acquaintance mentions these words in conversation, I take the emotional hit but continue listening and engaging in the conversation. It isn't their fault my brother is gone and theirs isn't .

I have heard many suicide loss survivors complain that they have lost friendships in the aftermath of the suicide. One reason for this sad occurrence is our friends may not know what to say. Death is a very uncomfortable topic, and suicide is even more so. I always try to be cognizant of my audience. I have a couple of good friends who have experienced many losses. They're excellent to talk to because they can relate to my pain and the subsequent emotions. They also know exactly what to say, having been on the receiving end. When it comes to the vast majority of my friends, I avoid talking about my brother unless they specifically ask a question about him. I have some friends who routinely ask how my parents and I are holding up, and I'll be honest with them. When they ask the question, I feel comfortable talking about Doug because they initiated the conversation. If they don't ask, I don't talk about him. I try not to get angry or take it personally. Avoidance is a common response to death. It doesn't mean they don't care; it simply means they don't know how to talk about it.

Initially at work, everyone was extremely cautious around me. There wasn't the normal banter. No one seemed to know how to act. I knew, in that moment, I needed to put everyone at ease. Just because my life had shattered didn't mean my entire team had to suffer with me. So I acted like my old self; I smiled, and I joked around. And within a couple days, everything returned to normal at work. The saying "fake it till you make it" was definitely at play here, but it served its purpose. I didn't want to be pitied or treated differently. Work became a respite from my personal life. It was a place where I could briefly escape the crippling grief I felt at home. It provided a much-needed distraction from the endless questions I had regarding Doug's suicide.

Lingering Questions

The most pressing question we have as suicide loss survivors is "Why?" Why did our loved ones feel they had no other choice but to end their lives? What led up to this decision? We have an understandable need to piece together their final days. Since we can't ask them, we turn to the limited options available to us.

I requested the autopsy report, police report, and pictures from the scene and autopsy. I wanted to know everything, so I began my own investigation. I read the autopsy report first, and it didn't tell me much that I didn't already know. The two big revelations were that Doug died instantly and that he was otherwise healthy. I was relieved to hear he didn't suffer physically, but I was upset reading about his perfectly healthy body. He threw it away! He could have gone on to live another fifty years. People with failing bodies fight to live, and Doug had a healthy body and fought to die. I couldn't wrap my mind around it.

I know now that Doug, despite his physical health, didn't have a healthy brain. He was just as sick as any terminal patient. Prior to Doug's death, I thought those who killed themselves were weak. I thought they took the easy way out. Now I see how utterly wrong that is. Those who take their own lives are strong. They're fighting demons we can't begin to imagine. But even the strong grow tired. People can only fight for so long before they can't fight anymore. Of course, the autopsy report couldn't tell me what Doug's final straw was, so I turned to the police report.

The police report was a major disappointment. I had hoped for eye-opening revelations, but instead I learned nothing new. There was no substance. The entire report was fewer than fourteen pages. This tragedy that turned my family's lives upside down was little more than a blip on the radar. Normally, I'm on the other side of investigations and I'm therefore privy to the unofficial theories that inevitably get bounced around. In this case, I was the victim, someone to be pitied and excluded from the informal conversation.

I had two discs full of pictures, and I assumed that they would help complete Doug's story. Before I had a chance to view them, I spoke to a good friend. I told her about the pictures I was going to look at later that day, and she asked a simple question: "Why?" Why would I do that to myself, and what did I hope to achieve? I paused, trying to come up with an intelligent answer and failing. I had already seen Doug at the funeral home. I wasn't in denial. The pictures would confirm that he was really dead, but I already knew that. I wasn't the one who found him—our parents did—so I didn't see him lying where he died. I'm not haunted by that final, traumatic image. If I saw the pictures, they couldn't be unseen. They would cause a considerable amount of harm for no apparent gain.

I'm fond of the common saying, "Just because you can doesn't mean you should." Although I don't always take this advice, I did when it came to the pictures. I thought I wanted to know everything surrounding Doug's death, but I began to see the wisdom in asking why. If I didn't have a good answer, then I stopped and re-evaluated.

I understand the burning desire to know everything about our loved one's life and death. It won't bring them back, but it gives us a purpose. Perhaps we think we can prevent future tragedies by fully understanding this one. We also may seek answers in the hope that it will eliminate some of our own guilt. Our loved ones made their choice, but it's easy to blame ourselves.

The last time I saw Doug, I was stressed out and dealing with a mold remediation company. He came over to my house because he wanted a sample of the mold to look at under his microscope. I had no idea why he was interested in doing that, and I really didn't care. My house was literally falling apart and walls were being torn down; I simply didn't have time to deal with my brother's odd request. I let him into my house but only said a few words to him before I turned my attention back to the workers. That was our last memory together. I tear up every time I think about it. If only I had known I would never see him again, I would have said and done everything so differently.

I know that Doug didn't kill himself because I was short with him that day, but it hurts nonetheless. A friend pointed out that the only reason I remember that last conversation so vividly is because it was the last. Doug surely understood that I was stressed out and didn't take it personally. When he pulled the trigger, I seriously doubt he was thinking about the last words we exchanged. In fact, I doubt he was thinking much about us at all. I don't think he could see beyond his pain. I believe he felt like a burden, and he thought he was doing us a favor. And as hard as it is to admit, I did feel some relief initially. I had worried about my brother for years. Although he had never attempted suicide before, he talked about it a lot. I didn't think he would really do it, but every time he was especially depressed, I worried. Every day I prayed to God that Doug wouldn't end his life. Looking back through our texts, I saw that I expressed my concern to him at least as early as 2016. At the time, he dismissed my worries and assured me he would never kill himself.

Did he know back then? Was he planning this for weeks, months, or even years? Or was it a spur of the moment decision? Was there anything we could have done to stop him? These are questions everyone has, and sadly, we will probably never know the answer. A small number of suicides are extremely well planned. They're carried out by meticulous individuals who buy life insurance and wait the necessary time for the suicide clause to expire, and they write long letters or journals detailing exactly why they made the choice they did. The vast majority do no such thing. These individuals leave no explanation behind. They may have been diagnosed with a mental illness, or there might have been no indication that anything was amiss.

Many people request the police and autopsy reports hoping they will fill in the blanks. That wasn't the end result for me, but that won't necessarily be the case for you. If you decide to obtain these reports, just be aware that they will be graphic. The autopsy report will be very exact as to how your loved one died.

My brother died by a self-inflicted gunshot wound to the head, but the report didn't stop there. It explained in detail the path the bullet took and the devastation left in its wake. I'm familiar with guns and I'm well aware of what a bullet can do, so the autopsy report wasn't terribly surprising to me. My mom was more upset by it, and I don't think she made it all the way through. If your loved one chose an especially traumatic method of suicide, the autopsy report will be more difficult to read.

The length of the police investigation will vary depending on the circumstances of the suicide and the jurisdiction. It took approximately four months for Doug's case to close. As far as the police report is concerned, there will be no theories or guesses. The report will contain the basic facts and nothing more. If you want to know if the suicide was planned over a long period of time, the police will generally not have an answer. If you want to know why your loved one chose to end their life, or why they chose a specific method, the police won't have those answers either. After I received Doug's report, I emailed the investigator because I was bothered by how sparse it was. He told me that unless I found a journal Doug wrote, I would probably never know the answers to my questions.

I already knew there wasn't a journal. I searched Doug's house three times after it was turned over to us. The first time was two days after Doug's body was found. I wanted to find a note, despite the fact that the police told us there wasn't one. I refused to believe Doug could have left us without saying goodbye. I went through everything as thoroughly as possible before I conceded that he really hadn't left one.

On that visit, I took sentimental items from his house. All of these items meant something to me, like the stuffed football he had made in junior high home-economics class, keychains with his name on them, and a license plate from the motorcycle he once owned. I was only his motorcycle passenger once, but I still remember clinging to him for dear life as he sped down the freeway. Everything I took now sits on his desk in my living room, as a memorial to him.

I also took his computer, hopeful it would contain some of his innermost thoughts. Unfortunately, it didn't. It did contain several papers he wrote during the previous year while he attended a community college, and I'm grateful I have them. He was a brilliant and funny writer, and I enjoy going back and rereading the papers.

While combing through his house, I was careful to avert my eyes when I walked by the spot where his body was found. The police cut out the carpet soaked in blood, but there was still blood spatter on the ceiling and the side of a cabinet. I wasn't ready to see it, and I certainly didn't want to picture him kneeling there in his final moments.

The next time I went through his house, it was to pick up specific items. I was also there to empty his fridge and turn off his heat. I took a few DVDs for myself, and I grabbed some items that his friends expressed interest in having.

The last time I went to Doug's house was the week before the closing. A local farmer wanted the land and was purchasing the house with the intention of bulldozing it. Under the circumstances, we all thought that was the best option. This visit was the most emotional. I went through everything again. This time, I took a jacket he got when he was in high school that he used to wear all the time. I still have a picture from twenty years ago of Doug wearing it on a family vacation in California. I also took a sweater that smelled like him. I looked at the blood spatter and cried. I knelt where he had knelt, and I imagined how he felt that night five months earlier when he made the decision to end his life. I choose to believe he felt peace and relief, knowing his pain was about to end. I'll never know how he actually felt, but that seems right. Did he feel fear as well? I hope not, but I suppose that's possible, if not probable.

Doug had a Ouija board. I noticed it on my first visit, and I felt a chill at the time as I looked at the "Goodbye" written in fancy lettering on the bottom. On this last visit, I pulled out the Ouija board. I had never touched one before. I placed it on the ground where Doug's body had lain, and I challenged him to move the planchette. I stared at it intently for a minute. Suddenly, I heard a loud knocking. I couldn't be sure where it was coming from. The door would have been the logical answer, but it sounded like it was coming from inside the house. I crouched down and pulled out my gun, which I routinely carried ever since discovering Doug's house had been broken into shortly after he was found. I strained to hear any further sounds. All was quiet.

Doug had thick plastic and sheets covering all the windows, and he didn't have a peephole in his door. I tried to look through the kitchen window, located next to the door, but everything was distorted through the plastic. However, I didn't see any movement. I then cleared the house. I had already rummaged through it, as if saying a silent goodbye to all the unclaimed items, so I was fairly certain there was no one else there. After clearing the house with negative results, I determined that it was either someone knocking on the door who slipped away before I looked out the window, or it was Doug playing a joke on me as I pathetically stared at his Ouija board. Either way, it was time to leave. As I started my car, I thought about a song from the '90s that Doug had loved and listened to over and over when we were in high school. Suddenly, that song came on the radio. I hadn't heard it in so long, and I wondered if it was Doug's doing. Tears streamed down my face as I drove away from Doug's house for the last time.

* * *

I want to take a moment to talk about the gun Doug used to end his life. We were all adamant in January that we wanted it destroyed. Over the ensuing months, I began having second thoughts. Doug's AR15 was his most prized possession. He put a nice scope on it, and I bought him a sling one year for Christmas. He shot it frequently, seeing how small he could get his groupings on the target.

During my second police academy in 2016, I struggled a lot with my rifle class. I was probably the only person in history to be more accurate with my handgun than my rifle. And that's not because I was phenomenal with a handgun; I was just that awful with a rifle. The instructors didn't know what to do with me. Doug offered to take me out so I could shoot his rifle to get some much-needed practice. I finally caught on toward the end of the class and passed the qualification, so I never took him up on that offer. Even though I never got to shoot with him, I knew how much he loved that gun.

The way I see it, the rifle didn't end Doug's life, Doug ended his life. The rifle was nothing more than a tool. It was also the last thing he touched, and that meant something to me. I realize there will be people reading this who will be appalled that I wanted to keep the tool my brother used to end his life. To this day, I have family members who believe Doug would still be alive if it weren't for that gun. There's no doubt in my mind that Doug would have found another way. I couldn't bear the thought of Doug's prized possession being destroyed, or worse, sold in an auction. He wouldn't want that, and neither did I. So I requested the rifle. I doubt I'll ever shoot it, but at least I'm taking care of it for my big brother.

The possessions you decide to keep are a personal choice. The only advice I'll give is to not make any hasty decisions. If it's something you know you'll never want, then by all means throw it away. I did this with Doug's Ouija board, and I have no regrets about that. If it's something you don't want now but think you might possibly want in the future, think long and hard before tossing it. The first time I went through Doug's house, I didn't think I wanted any of his clothing or furniture. Now my living room consists of Doug's desk, couch, and a puzzle that our dad put together and framed for Doug at his request. The room is more Doug than me, and it brings me great comfort. I would have regretted not taking these items, even though I was unsure at the time.

I'm glad I read the reports, even if they didn't give me the answers I was seeking. I'm equally glad I didn't look at the pictures. I prefer to know exactly how Doug died rather than leave it up to my imagination, but I also realize that seeing the pictures wouldn't have provided any additional answers. Others may prefer not to know the specifics, and that's perfectly fine. There's no right or wrong way to search for answers. Ultimately, you need to follow your heart and know your limits.

SUPPORT

During the first two weeks after Doug's death, I sought an online support group for suicide loss survivors. I found a Facebook group that had approximately 12,000 members when I joined, and it has grown considerably since. It was a relief knowing there were other people out there who were experiencing a similar grief and had the same unanswered questions. I didn't post much, but I read all the stories. One thing that shocked me was how many of the posters were suicidal themselves. There was so much despair that it probably wasn't healthy to read all the posts so early in my grief.

While perusing the online support group, I discovered something interesting. After Doug's death, I told my friends he committed suicide. I didn't realize at the time that saying "committed suicide" was a controversial term. I'm not one to argue semantics, and I'm certainly not concerned with being politically correct, but I came to see the wisdom of getting rid of this term. The reasoning is that "committed" has a negative connotation, as if our loved ones committed a crime. It implies that their action is something of which we should be ashamed.

The word I saw used instead perplexed me: *completed*. I took issue with this because of the positive connotation associated with the word completed. We complete work tasks and homework assignments. Completed implies that we did something good and should be proud of our success. To be fair, the full term isn't "completed suicide"; rather, it's "completed their life." The term isn't meant to celebrate the act of suicide. Regardless of the intent, I fear it does just that.

One of our goals as suicide loss survivors is to remove the stigma of suicide. That doesn't mean we should glamorize it. I prefer to say that I lost my brother to suicide. Just as we lose people to cancer and heart disease. It's a passive way of saying it, which subconsciously tells others that our loved one died of an illness. I don't say it with shame or with pride; it's merely a fact. When we lose loved ones to any physical illness, there's generally no judgement. Sometimes treatment simply does not work. Mental illness is no different, and hopefully in the near future it will be seen as such.

I also joined another online support group specifically for sibling suicide loss survivors. There are certainly many commonalities to all suicide losses. Whether we lose a sibling, a spouse, a parent, a child, a niece or nephew, or an aunt or uncle, many of our feelings are the same. However, there are some unique aspects specific to the relationship we lost. Many of those in my sibling group also understand what it's like to suddenly be an only child in their thirties. They understand the dread of knowing they will one day be older than their older siblings. They understand the crippling fear of taking care of aging parents by themselves and being completely alone after their parents pass. I strongly encourage fellow suicide loss survivors to join support groups, whether they're for all survivors or specific to a particular relationship. It's an excellent place to pose questions and receive guidance from those who have lived through a similar experience.

These two groups did help, but I was still struggling with depression. The realization that I would never see my brother again weighed heavily on me. Eternity is impossible to comprehend, and I felt like I was drowning. I was struggling with the regret over snapping at my brother the last time I saw him. The guilt and anger—toward both him and myself—was all consuming. I was not suicidal, but I was ambivalent about life.

I have always been a risk-taker, and I'm well aware I don't always make the smartest decisions. In an effort to change and be more responsible, I had given up skydiving approximately nine months earlier after a friend died in a skydiving accident. If it could happen to him, I reasoned, it could certainly happen to me. Even after more than 200 jumps, my landings were terrible. Now, suddenly, I had the urge to jump out of a plane again. And if I died, so be it. Concerned with this indifference to life, I decided to go to therapy instead.

Admittedly, therapy wasn't nearly as much fun as skydiving. However, I'll not say anything negative about therapy. I have heard from many people that it helped them tremendously. It just didn't help me much. It certainly didn't make anything worse, but I didn't walk away feeling any lighter or less troubled. Telling my story helped, but once I was done with that, I wasn't sure what else therapy could do for me. I went a total of three times, and then I stopped. Covid-19 was a convenient excuse, because all therapy sessions were being moved to virtual forums. If in-person therapy wasn't helping, I assumed that virtual therapy would be even worse.

Again, I want to reiterate that therapy is something everyone should try if they're struggling. In hindsight, the reason it didn't work for me is largely due to my job. I was afraid that if I were truly honest, I would potentially be deemed unfit for duty. If I had found another therapist who wasn't paid for by my department, I could have opened up more, and the outcome may have been different.

Therapy has and will continue to save lives, and its importance should never be downplayed.

During those three weeks in therapy, I looked online to see if there were any support groups for suicide loss survivors that met in person. I found a group that met once a month at a local hospital, and my therapist encouraged me to attend. I emailed the coordinator to make sure the meeting was still taking place later that month. I received a very warm and welcoming response, confirming that the group was, in fact, meeting. The response also stated that a local medium would be there for a group reading. I stared at the email in disbelief. Granted, I was new to support groups, but surely a medium wasn't standard practice. Right?

As I said before, I grew up in a Christian church, and I was well aware that we were prohibited from communicating with the dead. I was always the girl sitting alone at sleepovers while everyone else gathered around the Ouija board. Mediums were absolutely, positively out of the question. As I got older, I started having serious doubts about life after death. So while I wasn't necessarily against mediums for religious reasons anymore, I thought they were all frauds. I believed mediums simply took advantage of the bereaved, and the whole thing disgusted me. I understood the appeal of communicating with the deceased, but I was far too smart to fall for that scam!

I was intrigued though. What if . . . Doug wasn't really gone? What if his spirit was still here, ready and able to communicate with me? I did some research, and for every website praising mediumship, there were many others claiming it was a farce. I was very much on the fence. As I explained to my therapist, I really wanted to believe our spirits live on, but I had never seen any proof. I realize where there's no doubt, there can't be faith. But too much doubt makes faith equally impossible, and that's where I found myself. My faith was sinking in a sea of doubt. My therapist still thought I should go, and I acknowledged that I had nothing to lose. We didn't have to pay to attend, and I could, for the first time in my life, see a medium in action.

I had been grappling with the idea of spirits and ghosts long before Doug's death. Working in a jail, I have heard many ghost stories that intrigued me, but I was still doubtful. My only personal experience with "ghosts" had occurred while working the graveyard shift. I had heard some weird things, like cell doors closing even though none were open. But it was easy enough to dismiss that as my imagination working overtime. However, one experience in 2019 gave me pause because I actually felt it. A couple years prior, an inmate hung himself in his cell. Ever since, that cell door acted a bit funny. Most of the time, it worked as it should. We would hit the unlock button, and it would open a couple inches so that the occupant could manually open it the rest of the way if they wanted to enter or exit. On occasion, instead of opening those couple inches and staying open, the door would pop open and then immediately slam closed. I would excuse it as a combination of gravity and a mechanical glitch. I wasn't sure why it would only do that on rare occasions, but I'm hardly a mechanical engineer.

On this one particular night, an inmate was brought down to be housed in that cell. We radioed to have the door opened while we were walking to it. I heard the door open, but it slammed shut before we were able to reach it. No problem. I called for it again as I grabbed the handle, intending to guide it open. When the door opened, it tried to slam so hard the handle was nearly ripped out of my hand. I grabbed the door with both hands and threw my body weight into it, surprised by the amount of resistance I was experiencing. It felt exactly like there was someone on the other side of the door attempting to close it with great force. The struggle lasted about five seconds when, suddenly, the resistance was gone and the door flew open. Almost as if someone let go of the door. But no one was there. To this day, I'm not really sure what transpired. Could it have been some kind of mechanical problem? Perhaps. Could it be coincidental that this has only occurred in the cell where someone hung himself? Sure. I did discover after the fact that the inmate who hung himself had slammed the door shut before taking his life, much like how the door slams shut now. But it could still be a coincidence.

* * *

I arrived at my first suicide loss survivors meeting in mid-March with trepidation. I was nervous to be around other survivors. I was afraid I'd break down, and they would judge me. I was equally afraid I wouldn't break down, and they'd judge me for that as well. I wanted to turn around and run. I wasn't ready for this. I wanted to go home and cry myself to sleep, as I did most nights. But the promise of the medium propelled me forward. What were the odds that the first meeting I decided to attend would have a medium? I felt like it was meant to be, and so I went.

There were roughly ten of us. We were on the cusp of the Covid-19 pandemic, but we shook hands, and no one wore masks. We went around the table, introducing ourselves and briefly stating why we were there. A mother and daughter duo had lost their grandson/son. Two men lost their wives. A young woman lost her friend. A man lost his grandson. A woman lost her son. Another woman lost her brother. There were a lot of tears, but they had dried up by the time another woman entered the room. Her name was Kim Moore, and she was like a ray of sunshine. Her personality sparkled, and she lit up the room. For some reason, this was not how I envisioned a medium.

Kim explained how the whole process would work. I was very skeptical, but hopeful nonetheless. I was wearing my necklace with Doug's ashes in it, as if Kim was a bloodhound who could sniff out his spirit if I wore something of his. Kim stated that there were many spirits present, and the first one coming through was a father figure belonging to someone on my side of the room. I inwardly rolled my eyes. I was willing to bet every single person in the room could claim that spirit as their loved one. The skeptic in me was winning. One woman established that it was likely her father. He hadn't killed himself and wasn't the reason she was there. Everything the medium said about him was generic, and I felt like I had made a big mistake in coming. But it wasn't as if I could leave in the middle of the reading, so I sat back and listened.

The next spirit to come through was the young woman's friend. The medium said the spirit was showing her curly hair. The woman teared up and said that her friend always curled her hair. There were a few other details that were just specific enough it grabbed my attention. This medium was a good guesser!

The son/grandson of the mother and grandmother came through, along with an older man. Kim frowned in confusion, and said there was something wrong with the order. The boy died first, perhaps? The grandmother responded that her grandson died, and then her father, the grandson's great-grandfather, followed a few weeks later. That was interesting. If I were going to guess, I certainly would have said that the boy's great-grandfather likely preceded the boy in death. She had my undivided attention now. The medium told the mother that she slept with something of her son's, and every time she hugged it to her chest, his spirit felt the hug in heaven. The woman began sobbing and said she had her son's shirt wrapped around a pillow, and she hugged it to her chest every night as she slept. I could feel my skepticism start to slip away. One of the last things she said was that the boy liked to turn the TV off while his sisters were watching it because he thought it was funny. We all chuckled. Little did I know how important that detail would prove to be in my own journey.

Several other spirits came through, and the last one was a man's wife. Through the medium, she told him to stop reading the note because she didn't mean any of it except the part that said "I love you." With tears streaming down his face, he said that she left a suicide note for him, and he had read it every day for the last twelve years looking for answers. I was blown away. As I pointed out before, the majority of suicides don't leave notes. Not only did this medium know his wife left a note, she knew he had read it repeatedly. Once again, the details were so specific I simply couldn't deny that there was something special about Kim. She got everything right.

When Kim announced the end of the session, I was crushed. I had been silently chanting my brother's name for the past half hour, hoping to conjure him. Before she left, Kim looked directly at me and said if our loved ones were shy in life, they wouldn't come through during a group reading. She set her business cards on the table and left. I pondered that as the meeting finished up. Doug was extremely shy and introverted. Obviously, mediums make far more for a private session than for a group reading, so naturally Kim would try to push for more business. It was like she had dangled a carrot in front of me. Normally I wouldn't have taken the bait, but she was so incredibly accurate. Nothing about her seemed fake. She genuinely appeared to be speaking with our deceased loved ones. I snatched a card and left the meeting.

Hope

Everything changed for me after seeing a medium at work. My deep depression was replaced by something new: hope. Although Doug hadn't come through during the group reading, I had hope for the first time in two months that I may hear from him again. I had hope that our story together hadn't ended; it had merely changed shape. My instinct was to schedule a private session with Kim, but I was nervous. I was absolutely terrified that Doug wouldn't come through, and it would be like losing him all over again. What if I paid for an hour-long session, only to have no one come through? I wondered if mediums offered refunds.

After talking it over with friends, I decided to go for it. I scheduled an appointment for three weeks out. That night, I wrote to Doug and threatened to kick his butt if he didn't show up. My bedroom light flickered in response. I was mesmerized. Could it be that he was actually there listening to me? Were all these letters actually being read by him? I wasn't completely convinced, but I was confident enough to keep the appointment.

While I was waiting for the reading, I went back to the basics to cope with my grief. I forced myself to get out of bed every day, even if it was just to walk downstairs to the couch. Always an avid runner, I got back on the treadmill. I continued going to work.

A few days after scheduling with the medium, I was on my treadmill and simultaneously watching TV, which was located across the room. It suddenly turned off. I was puzzled. I wasn't touching the remote, and there wasn't a power outage or surge. Everything else stayed on, but the screen was black. I turned the TV back on with a shrug and finished my run.

It took an embarrassingly long time for me to make the connection between my TV's mysterious behavior and Kim's words to the mother during the group reading. Kim had told the woman that her son liked to turn the TV off while his sisters were watching it. Once I remembered that, I was convinced Doug had been present for the reading. He hadn't come forward, but he was listening. I smiled, imagining Doug pulling the son aside after the reading and asking the son to show him how to play the same trick on me. That provided some comfort and humor, and further reassured me that I would hear from Doug during the medium reading.

Over the next couple weeks, the pandemic changed everything. Most states, including Colorado, shut down. Although it really didn't affect my day-to-day life, it did affect my medium appointment. I had planned to see the medium in person, but that was no longer possible. I was informed I could either switch to a phone appointment or reschedule once the state reopened. Waiting was simply not an option. I felt that Doug had agreed to be there on that date, and changing it would violate our "agreement." Of course, that's not really how mediumship works, but I was so anxious that I wasn't thinking rationally.

I researched medium phone readings and discovered that most mediums claim phone sessions are more accurate because they can't see their client's face. They're able to focus more on the spirits, rather than scrutinizing our reactions. I still wasn't sure how it was possible for the medium to communicate with spirits if we weren't in the same room, but I had no other choice. It also provided a plausible excuse for me if Doug didn't come through. I could blame the method rather than admit he was truly gone.

On April 2, I was a nervous wreck. I wrote to Doug shortly before the afternoon reading, pleading with him to show up. If he didn't, I was worried I would never recover. In that moment, I realized the only thing keeping me going was my belief that his spirit was still with me. I would never see him again or have a normal conversation with him, but if I could have some evidence that he was still with me, it would make his physical absence a little easier to bear. If he didn't come through, I would have to come to terms with the very real possibility that he was gone forever. To give myself an out, I decided instead to wait another six months and try again if I failed to connect that day. I had to have some hope to grasp, or I would drown.

Kim was running a little late, and I was clutching Doug's necklace with one hand and my phone with the other. After what felt like an eternity, the phone finally rang. I answered, and Kim quickly got down to business. She explained that the session would be recorded, and the recording would be sent to me later. Then she stated there were several spirits present if I was ready to get started. I breathlessly said I was.

The first two spirits to come through could have been my grandparents. Honestly, the information was so vague, they could have been anyone. I tried to fight the disappointment I felt, but doubt was creeping in. Then Kim informed me that the female spirit had another, younger male with her. It was Doug!

I would love to detail the reading verbatim, because even the staunchest skeptics would have to admit Kim was eerily accurate. There was no conceivable way she could possibly know the things she knew, including the falling out he had with his good friend. However, my promise to keep Doug's story private outweighs my desire to convince skeptics. I can't repeat everything Doug told me that day because it was far too personal. He explained his actions, he said he is at peace now, and he told me he's proud of me and he loves me.

I can also tell you how I felt after the conclusion of the reading. I believe, almost without a doubt, that Doug's spirit lives on. I believe there is nothing I could have done or said to prevent Doug's death. The reading enabled me to go inside his mind and see how much he was suffering. The closure and relief were immediate. There was no more confusion or anger on my part, just acceptance and sadness. I'll feel this sadness and pain for the rest of my life, but I'm willing to carry that burden if it means Doug is no longer suffering. I don't have to like what happened to accept it. I'm forever grateful to Kim for helping me connect with Doug. I don't know where I'd be if it weren't for her.

My goal in detailing my experience is to offer hope, not to drum up business for mediums. If seeing a medium is against your religious beliefs or something in which you have no interest, I'll not try to convince you otherwise. I respect your beliefs, and I sincerely hope you find another way to get the closure we're all seeking.

I mention my experience with a medium because this is quite possibly the most common question I see in my online support groups. People are inherently curious about life after death, and it becomes much more pressing once we lose someone close to us. Seeing a medium is a frightening prospect for many and every experience—good or bad—is helpful for those on the fence. For those leaning toward seeing a medium, please do your research first. I'm a believer in mediums, but I also know there are fraudulent mediums pretending to have a gift in order to make some easy money. We're more vulnerable when we're hurting, and I don't want anyone to fall victim to these scammers.

There are some people who are adamant that death is the end, and others who are just as adamant that spirits live forever, but most of us are somewhere in the middle. We want to believe our loved ones are with us, but our logical minds insist this isn't possible. We will never fully know the answer until we leave this earth, but I'd rather believe in an afterlife and be wrong than lose hope altogether.

Ultimately, I don't know how I would survive my brother's death without believing in the possibility of being reunited with him someday. The alternative is too horrible to contemplate, and I'm not sure why anyone would voluntarily choose to do so. I'll never judge those who disagree with me, but I do feel sadness for them. If we can't know something for certain—and obviously we can't in this case or there would be no debate—then why not choose the option that will give us peace? I know I've overly simplified a very complex subject, but sometimes the simplest answer is the best answer. Humans often complicate things unnecessarily, and we bring misery upon ourselves in the process. When it comes to the afterlife debate, I'll always choose hope.

Turning Point

I would love to say that the medium session was the end of my grief, but it most certainly was not. I was elated for a few days, especially as I began to see and recognize signs from Doug. I can't be sure, of course, that they were truly signs, but I chose to believe they were. Electronics turned on and off, and my smoke detector chirped once when I wasn't even cooking! I knew logically these signs could have been mere coincidences; indeed, looking back, I'm positive some of them were. But others absolutely felt like Doug, and I took great comfort from that.

The elation gave way to a more disturbing feeling: anguish. I realized that talking to Doug through Kim was quite possibly the last time I would "hear" from him, and that made me feel sick. I could accept that he wasn't physically here anymore, but I couldn't accept that I would never talk to him again. I couldn't stand the thought of never having something to look forward to regarding Doug. In the same way that I always schedule my annual vacation for the end of the year so that the anticipation will help me make it through all the other months, I needed something to help me make it through life without Doug. I needed something to anticipate and get excited about.

I immediately decided that I would schedule another medium reading for six months or so in the future. I considered the possibility that I would be disturbing him, but I didn't care. He owed it to me, after all. It was the least he could do after leaving me without a sibling.

I began second guessing my decision as I wrote to Doug that night. What did I hope to achieve from another reading? I got all the answers I was seeking regarding his suicide and mindset at the time. I felt a sense of peace. Doug was okay, he loved me, and he was far happier there (wherever there was) than he had ever been here. There was nothing left for him to say.

I made the heartbreaking choice to let Doug go. I was selfish in thinking he owed me anything. He had already explained his actions. The only thing I would get from future readings was more corroboration that his spirit was still with me. Any doubt at all concerns me greatly. I want to know beyond a shadow of a doubt that Doug is still here—and I'll never have that. It isn't possible for those on earth to know for certain what happens after death. Even seeing Doug's ghost wouldn't be conclusive. Nothing will ever be enough. I realized that I needed to have faith, and faith can only exist where there's doubt.

* * *

I had two visitation dreams following Kim's reading, and they were amazing. I don't think they would have been possible without Kim. Visitation dreams are believed to be actual visits by spirit. It's easier for spirit to visit us when we're unconscious and therefore unable to object to what our rational minds believe can't be true. This is also why mediums say children and animals are more sensitive to ghostly visits. They're far more open-minded than we are and can see things they *shouldn't* be able to see.

Visitation dreams are common, but the timing of them depends on where you are with your grief. Seeing Kim and realizing Doug's spirit lives on was instrumental in opening this door for me. I was able to let go of my anger and accept Doug's passing, which likely enabled me to receive his visits.

I can't say without a doubt that visitation dreams are real and that this phenomenon is what I experienced. I do know these dreams made me feel so much better, especially after the euphoria of Kim's reading wore off. I choose to believe that Doug really did visit me. This belief has helped me heal, and it does me no harm. As I've said, I'd rather believe and be wrong than have no hope at all.

In addition to the dreams, I had one other occasion during which I believe Doug visited. This time, it wasn't in a dream. It occurred in my bedroom after I had awoken from a dream. I was asleep when a sound like a gunshot startled me. I sat up immediately, trying to ascertain if the noise was real or if I had dreamed it. Suddenly, I felt a heaviness that's difficult to explain. It was as if my room was electrically charged. I saw what looked like a hazy glow coming from the far corner of my room, but I wasn't wearing my contacts so everything was fuzzy. As I was trying to make sense of what I was seeing and feeling, Zoey began thrashing around in her sleep. She then began growling, which scared me. And just as suddenly as it started, it abruptly stopped, and my room returned to normal. I don't know if that was truly Doug, but I like to think it was. I haven't felt that heavy energy since, but I keep hoping it will reoccur someday.

* * *

Despite my promise to Doug not to see another medium, I would do so approximately five months later. After my in-person support group meeting in March, when I was introduced to Kim, our meetings got moved to Zoom courtesy of Covid-19. I'm technologically challenged and had no interest in figuring out how Zoom worked. However, I received an email in September regarding that month's meeting, and I saw that another medium would be featured. Her name was Danielle, and I was intrigued. Were all mediums essentially the same, or would I learn something new about mediumship and the afterlife?

I reluctantly downloaded Zoom on my phone and gave myself a little tutorial. I wrote to Doug and told him I wasn't expecting him to come through. I told him I was doing fine and just wanted to watch another medium at work. I also thought it would be comforting merely seeing the readings that others got. It wouldn't specifically corroborate the existence of Doug's spirit but perhaps the afterlife in general.

I signed into the meeting that night and listened to the other member's introductions. There was roughly a dozen of us, and several had never had a medium reading before. Many were distraught, and I silently told Doug not to come through so that their loved ones would have a chance. They needed it more than me.

Danielle virtually entered the meeting after the introductions. She is a renowned medium, and I was excited to meet her. She explained how the process worked, and it was similar to Kim's spiel. We then got started with the first spirit, who was a generic mother figure, and the other members tried to figure out if it was their loved one. I quickly remembered why group readings aren't ideal. I was sitting back in my chair, confident that I would be nothing more than a spectator this time. After the first spirit, Danielle called me out by name and asked what man would be there for me. Startled, I fumbled with my phone and managed to unmute my microphone. I croaked out, "My brother." Danielle patiently asked for his name, and I told her it was Doug.

Danielle nodded and started off by stating that Doug wouldn't normally do a group reading, but he thought it was actually kind of cool. That was exactly what I would expect Doug to say. Danielle then went on to say essentially the same things Kim had said. I was thrilled to hear from Doug, but I was also oddly disappointed. This confounded me. Here was this second medium corroborating what the first medium told me, and I was disappointed! In the time between Kim's reading and Danielle's reading, I felt like I was on the same wavelength as Doug. I was seeing signs everywhere and had visitation dreams. I felt completely connected to him. So how could it be that Doug came through when I was positive he wouldn't? It called into question everything that happened over the past five months. Were those signs even from him? I had felt peace and excitement after Kim's reading, but I felt almost despondent after Danielle's.

The group reading was derailed by a woman who was clearly a disbeliever and began arguing with everything Danielle said. The woman was distraught over the suicide of her father, and Danielle was trying to help her but got rather frustrated by the woman's outright hostility. Regardless of whether you believe in the afterlife or mediumship, please don't behave the way this woman did during a group reading. It's perfectly fine to be skeptical and to have questions, but becoming verbally combative with the medium hurts everyone. Aside from making us all uncomfortable, it tainted our own readings. It took the focus off our loved ones and placed it on the spectacle unfolding in front of us.

In the end, I don't regret attending the Zoom meeting. Ultimately, Danielle's reading made me feel that she and Kim had truly communicated with Doug. Their readings were too similar to be coincidental, and they knew specific details they couldn't have guessed. I'm at a point now where I don't feel the need to seek out another medium. If one happens to be at a support-group meeting, I'll make an effort to attend. I do find mediumship fascinating, and I have a great deal more hope now than I did in the immediate aftermath of Doug's death. Seeing the mediums may not have been the end of my grief journey, but it certainly was the turning point. Up until then, I had barely been putting one foot in front of the other. After seeing Kim, and then Danielle, I felt my life slowly return to some semblance of normal. Rather than merely surviving, I started living again.

Faith Crisis

As a Christian, I was raised to believe in heaven and hell. The rules were fairly simple. Don't sin, and if you do, repent. Ask for forgiveness. And, of course, believe in God, Jesus, and the Holy Spirit. If you do those things, you'll spend eternity in heaven. If not, you'll go to the fiery pits of hell.

As I got older, I started having doubts about the logic of this. Would God really send a spirit to hell for all eternity for a minor offense? Are all offenses considered the same in His eyes? Is stealing really as bad as murder? I was able to table these questions for many years, but Doug's death brought them front and center.

Without going into detail, Doug was involved in some illegal drug activities. In my eyes, he wasn't a bad person. He had a big heart and a sensitive soul. He cared deeply for his friends and animals. He didn't have much money, but he was generous with what little he had. He would buy his friends' kids birthday and Christmas presents, and he donated to causes he believed in. In many ways, he was a better person than I am. He gave people the benefit of the doubt, whereas I'm overly cynical. Although Doug refused to see a psychologist and was never diagnosed with a mental illness, I truly believe Doug's drug-related illegalities were his way of self-medicating and helping others do the same. I don't say this to excuse his behavior, but I do believe it's an accurate explanation for his actions.

Nonetheless, Doug did sin. Without repentance, he couldn't be in heaven according to the Bible. Then there's the act of suicide itself. Although the Bible may not make mention of suicide specifically, murder is a sin. I always assumed suicide would be seen in the same light by God. And if Doug's very last act was killing himself, how could he have possibly repented?

More importantly, Doug didn't believe in God or Jesus. He and I had a conversation about that at one point. He believed there might be a god, but didn't believe in the Christian God. And he scoffed at the idea of Jesus as the Messiah. Everything I knew about the Bible and Christianity said that Doug would be damned to hell if he didn't believe.

I was perplexed by this. If I had actually communicated with Doug's spirit through Kim (and later, Danielle), and I believed I had, then he most certainly wasn't in hell. From what he described, it sounded an awful lot like he was in heaven. But how could that be? He had sinned and didn't believe in God. How could he possibly be in heaven?

This caused me quite a bit of distress. Either hell didn't exist, or I hadn't really communicated with Doug. The latter was inconceivable, so I assumed the former must be true. However, I quickly concluded that I couldn't really be a Christian if I didn't believe in hell. For that matter, I wasn't entirely sure heaven existed either. How could Doug be both there and here? But he had to be here because of all the signs he was sending me.

I began searching high and low for a religion that would fit my parameters. A religion where heaven maybe existed, but hell definitely didn't. And the religion absolutely had to believe in an afterlife. Not reincarnation though, because that was far too mind-boggling. My brain couldn't even comprehend the logistics of that, so it was out of the question.

In case it's not apparent, I was having a crisis. Even though I had lost some faith over the years, I still considered myself a Christian. It was part of my identity. There were parts of the religion I didn't agree with, but I believed in God and figured the rest would fall into place eventually. Suddenly, "eventually" was no longer acceptable. I needed answers, and I needed them now.

Most religions failed at least one of my strict requirements. The closest religion I could find was Judaism. I liked that they believed in annihilation rather than hell—it's more humane that way—but I wasn't terribly fond of their ambivalence about the afterlife. My studies led me to the conclusion that Judaism is focused more on the here and now and doesn't concern itself with what happens after death. That made me a little uneasy, but

I reasoned that the afterlife must exist in order for Doug to be communicating with me. I was able to push my concerns aside and order the Torah, my first step towards conversion.

One of my biggest obstacles was Covid-19. All synagogues were closed, so meeting with a rabbi in person to discuss my potential conversion wasn't an option. In fact, finding a local synagogue was a challenge in and of itself. I then began to have anxiety over the thought of adapting to a new culture, meeting new people, and learning what, exactly, eating kosher entailed.

Then there was the issue of Christmas. I absolutely adore the holiday. I love everything about it, and there was simply no way I could ever stop celebrating Christmas. But it seemed kind of odd to convert to a new religion, only to carry over all the traditions from my old religion. Why convert if I wasn't going to assimilate?

At this point, I decided to seek professional help from a trusted chaplain. I was in over my head and realized I wasn't acting particularly sane. So I spoke to the chaplain for several hours. When I told him that I refuse to believe

Doug is in hell despite what the Bible says, he gently reminded me that we can't know anyone else's heart. I may think Doug didn't believe in God or Jesus, but I can't know that for sure.

After speaking with the chaplain, I concluded that no religion will ever be perfect. And that's okay. Religion doesn't have to fit in a tidy box. I'm still a Christian, but I'm more spiritual than religious. Despite my little crisis, Doug's death helped me rediscover my faith. When it comes to suicide loss, it's common to either lose faith or find it. We get to choose which path to follow.

Unhappy Birthdays

My birthday, July 8, was the day after Doug's house was sold. I was oddly depressed that his house was no longer ours. It wasn't as if I went there often, but I liked having the option. I felt closer to him there. It was where he had died, true, but it was also where he had lived. The fact that my birthday immediately followed the sale added insult to injury.

For my birthday, I got takeout cheesecake from The Cheesecake Factory. Dining in still wasn't an option due to Covid-19. I stopped by the restaurant and ordered four pieces of cheesecake, and then I took them over to my parents' house. I fully understood that there were only three of us now, and I knew Doug's spirit wasn't going to grab a fork and dig in. It was symbolic, a gesture meant for him as well as me. We had always been a family of four, and I wasn't going to let Doug's death stand in the way of that.

My birthday was fine. We hung out in the backyard and watched Zoey run the length of the fence every time a motorcycle drove by. We talked and laughed and ate cheesecake. I tried to distract myself from the fact that I wouldn't be getting a call from Doug. For the first time in my thirty-five years, I was spending my birthday without my big brother. I searched high and low for a sign from Doug. Surely he would know how much I needed him, and he would let me know he was near. But I didn't get a sign that day, and it devastated me.

I was relieved when my birthday was over, but the relief was short-lived. What would have been Doug's thirty-seventh birthday was on July 30. When we were young, we had joint birthday parties. I liked to joke that our parents had us in the same month specifically so they could save money by only throwing one party. It didn't bother me, though. We invited our own friends and always did something fun.

Whereas my birthday had been tolerable, Doug's was excruciating. I cried a lot in the days leading up to, and including, his birthday. My mom gave me Doug's baby book so that I could go through it, and I did the night before his birthday. I read descriptions of him as a happy child and cried. I saw all our annual pictures sitting on Santa's lap, and I was sobbing so hard I could hardly breathe. How could he go from a happy, grinning boy, to someone who voluntarily ended his life at thirty-six years old?

Initially, we had planned to go up to the mountains where Doug and our dad used to hunt and scatter his ashes on his birthday. At the funeral home back in January, when we saw Doug for the last time, we also picked out an oak urn with a picture of mountains and an elk etched into the side. It truly was beautiful, but I did have to wonder why my parents would buy such a nice urn for ashes they planned to scatter. However, because Doug was 6'5", not all of his ashes fit in the urn. I suggested that we only scatter the ashes that wouldn't fit and keep the rest in the urn. My parents agreed. Due to the generally bad weather in the Rocky Mountains in the winter, we thought it would be wise to wait until summer.

The closer we got to Doug's birthday, the more my dad questioned whether we should scatter the ashes. I was okay with either option. Doug's spirit wasn't contained in the ashes after all. But I could see that my dad wasn't okay with letting his son go, so we decided that I would also get an urn and put the rest of the ashes in there. I found an urn I liked when I browsed online. It was oak as well, but this one had an eagle flying over the mountains. It felt like an appropriate choice because Doug had loved birds.

When Doug was young, he wanted to be a bird. He had a blue parakeet named Feathers, and I got a yellow one I named Chirpy. He believed flying was the ultimate freedom. In fact, he's the one who got me involved in skydiving. He bought me a gift certificate for indoor skydiving one Christmas, and because I didn't want to go alone, I bought him one for his following birthday. We also got our dad a gift certificate on Father's Day so we could all make fools out of ourselves together.

We finally went in July 2013, and none of us were naturals. But I got hooked. It really was like flying, and I fell in love with the potential. I kept going to the tunnel, and eventually I transitioned to real skydiving. Doug had always wanted to jump out of a plane, and we both went on a tandem skydive in early 2014. It was my third and Doug's first, and I'm so glad we got to experience that together. Doug loved it, but while I went on to get my license, Doug didn't have the time or the money to go through the accelerated freefall program.

So the eagle on the urn seemed perfect. It would have been a wonderful memorial. However, I just couldn't bring myself to buy it. I'm not sure why I resisted so much. Perhaps it seemed too final or too permanent. On Doug's birthday, months after deciding to keep the ashes, I finally worked up the courage to buy it. It arrived a week later and now sits on the coffee table in my living room.

* * *

Early in my grief, I thought about getting a memorial tattoo. I scheduled an appointment for July 30, as it seemed like a perfect way to mark Doug's birthday. I saw many posts online from fellow survivors showcasing their tattoos. Many incorporated a semicolon, and that piqued my curiosity. My research revealed that these semicolons mean the individuals chose to continue their lives rather than end them, much like an author uses a semicolon to continue a sentence. I understood the symbolism, but I was puzzled nonetheless. A semicolon made sense for someone who once considered ending their own life and instead chose to live. That would be a powerful reminder of their strength and commitment to keep going no matter what obstacles and hardships they faced. A semicolon is a perfect symbol for suicide prevention.

The problem I saw was that Doug didn't choose to continue his life. He didn't use a semicolon, so to speak. He used a period. I have to admit that I still don't fully understand why suicide loss survivors frequently have a semicolon somewhere in the tattoo. That's not to say these tattoos aren't wonderful, and indeed some are very clever in how they incorporate the semicolon. I simply don't understand them in this context. Do we wish our loved ones had punctuated their lives with a semicolon rather than a period? Of course we do. But they didn't. Perhaps the semicolon is a reminder for the tattoo recipients to continue on with their lives despite the intense grief they're enduring. Maybe it's a reminder for them to keep going despite their loss.

Regardless of the reasoning behind it, I couldn't get on board with Doug's tattoo having a semicolon. I felt like I was expected to incorporate it, given my status as a suicide loss survivor, but it didn't feel right to me. At the end of the day, a tattoo is a permanent alteration of your body. If a semicolon feels right to you, then certainly go for it. The important thing is that it has meaning for you; my opinion of anyone else's tattoo is irrelevant.

At first I tried designing a fancy tattoo that said "For you I shall live." I wanted Doug's name and date of birth and death. This was problematic, however. The tattoo placement was important. Although I liked the idea of getting it on my inner forearm, I didn't want it visible when I was in uniform. The last thing I wanted were inmates asking me who Doug was. My back would have been a good location considering the size this tattoo was shaping up to be. But if it was on my back, I wouldn't be able to see it. That defeated the purpose. Finally, I decided on my left ankle.

No matter how hard I tried, I knew I couldn't fit my original tattoo on my ankle. I also had some misgivings about the saying. It was catchy, but it wasn't very fitting for my relationship with Doug. He preferred to keep things simple, and I started seeing the wisdom in that. I settled for simply having his name and date of birth and death.

That led me to another major problem. I didn't know Doug's date of death. He was found on January 26, but he didn't die that day. In Colorado, the official date on the death certificate is the date that death is pronounced, regardless of when the individual actually died. The coroner couldn't tell us exactly when Doug died, but he concluded that he was lying there for at least two days. That would put his date of death on January 23—the last time anyone spoke to him—or January 24. For someone who places a huge importance on dates, this discrepancy bothered me a great deal. What if I put the wrong date on my ankle? Granted, I would never know for sure if the date was right or wrong, but the mere possibility that it could be wrong was almost unimaginable. Would I look at my ankle in disgust because I decided a moment too late that the other date was more accurate?

I posed this question to other survivors, and I received one suggestion in particular that I especially liked. Instead of exact dates, why not use years instead? I played around with that, and I was perfectly content using only 2020 as the date of death. However, I really wanted his full date of birth in the tattoo. I was tempted to have the tattoo read "7/30/83–2020," but that felt too asymmetrical. I realized I needed to pick a date and hope for the best. Because January 23 was Doug's last known communication, I chose that date. In all reality, the date has never bothered me since it was tattooed on my skin. If it said the 24th, I would have been fine with that as well. My advice for those in similar situations is to go with your gut. As long as it feels right to you, that's all that matters.

The most important part of the tattoo was that everything would be in Doug's writing. He had a unique way of writing his name, and I wanted that captured on my skin forever. I flirted with the idea of having some of his ashes mixed in with the ink, but I wasn't entirely comfortable with that. My dad had some of Doug's paperwork, and he scanned the documents into his computer and copied and pasted his name and individual numbers to create the tattoo. It was perfect. It looked exactly like Doug had made the tattoo himself, and I couldn't wait to have it inked onto my skin.

On July 30, I got the tattoo. I have another tattoo from fifteen years prior on my opposite ankle, so I wasn't terribly concerned about the pain. Either my pain tolerance has decreased or I didn't accurately remember my last experience, but I was extremely glad I didn't go with a bigger, more elaborate tattoo. The session only lasted about fifteen minutes, but the pain was much worse than I anticipated. People who spend hours at a time getting a tattoo have my utmost respect! My tattoo simply reads:

Doug Hoffmann
7/30/83–1/23/20

Everything, including the slashes and dash, are in his writing, and I love it. It's simple, yet it reminds me of him every time I look at it. To others, it's a small tattoo they barely register;

to me, it's part of my brother that I carry with me everywhere. It was the perfect way to spend his first heavenly birthday.

Searching for Purpose

Between our birthdays was another important milestone: the six-month anniversary of Doug's death. July 23–26 was going to be difficult. It was almost incomprehensible that I had lived for six months without my brother. In some ways, it felt like yesterday. In others, it felt like a lifetime. The entire month of July was so taxing and stressful that I knew I needed to get away for a few days. So I went to Yellowstone, my favorite destination. I was hoping to get lost in the beauty and spend some time alone with my thoughts.

I go to Yellowstone at least twice a year, and one of my underlying goals—obsessions, really—is to see one particular geyser. Steamboat Geyser is the world's tallest active geyser, and it's my holy grail. I have been pursuing it for years and keep missing it by mere hours. The geyser erupts every three days to fifty years, but it has been relatively frequent in recent years. It was "due" to erupt on July 23 or 24, and I thought that would be a great way to spend an otherwise difficult couple of days.

After leaving Zoey with my parents, I drove north towards Wyoming. As strange as it sounds, I felt like Doug was with me on the drive up. Doug worked for Sherwin-Williams for several years, and I saw two different Sherwin-Williams trucks drive directly in front of me. It could be that I'm extremely unobservant, but I don't recall ever seeing a Sherwin-Williams truck before. Suddenly, I saw two, and they were in unlikely places. The first was in northern Colorado, and it was driving on an overpass as I drove on the freeway below. The second was at a gas station outside of Rawlins, Wyoming. As I filled up my tank, the truck drove by on a side street. The first truck made me smile at the sweet coincidence. The second made me consider the implications. I had never seen a truck like this before, and now I saw two in the space of a few hours. They drove perpendicularly in front of me so I couldn't miss them no matter how oblivious I was. I took this as a sign, and I was so happy.

As I drove along a scenic byway, I began playing a Three Days Grace CD that Doug and I both loved. As the first song started playing, my body grew ice cold, and I started tingling from head to toe. I have had goosebumps before, as we all have, but this was an experience like no other. They say you get goosebumps when a spirit is near. I never put much stock in that, but at that moment, I felt like Doug was right there. The tingling and goosebumps lasted for a couple of minutes, and then they instantly disappeared along with the chill. To this day I have never had a repeat of that experience, but I remember it vividly.

I generally go to Yellowstone through the south entrance, which requires a drive through Grand Teton National Park. I almost always go during the shoulder months, May and October, to avoid the crowds, and I have never once been stopped at the entrance of Grand Teton. I have never even seen it manned, but it was on this trip. As I pulled up to the gate, the ranger asked, "Are you guys going to Yellowstone?" He then said "you guys" once more during our interaction. I smiled broadly. I was alone in the car, but was I really? I had felt Doug's presence for much of the drive, and the ranger seemed to unwittingly confirm it. Doug and I hadn't been to Yellowstone together for several years, and I was thrilled to have him join me on this trip.

I checked into my hotel in West Yellowstone that night and got an early start the following morning, July 22. I stopped by Steamboat to make sure it hadn't gone off earlier than expected, and then I explored the Porcelain Basin. It was so desolate, as much of Yellowstone is, and I loved the solitude. As one young boy walked past me, he remarked to his parents that the scenery looked so lonely. It really did, but that wasn't a negative to me. It was the perfect place to reflect on the past six months and to contemplate the future. I take comfort from the incredible history of Yellowstone, and the knowledge that it has been around for millions of years and will still be here long after I've passed.

I had been thinking a lot about the purpose of life since Doug left us. Was his purpose to suffer? Was my parents' purpose to create and nurture a child, only to have him take his own life at the age of thirty-six? Was my purpose to grieve my brother for the rest of my life?

From a purely logical standpoint, I would say the ultimate purpose of life is to make a contribution to society and to leave behind a legacy. Most people do so by procreating. What better way to contribute than by creating life and raising the next generation to be productive members of society? After all, procreating is necessary to humanity's survival.

So what happens when the life you created ends prematurely? Parents sacrifice so much to give their progeny a good start in life. I watched my parents nearly lose their minds dealing with Doug's teenage antics. They paid for our sports, braces, first cars, college classes, rent, and so much more just to give us every opportunity for success. Was all that a waste considering how Doug's life had ended? If children are our purpose, then it stands to reason that losing a child is akin to losing your purpose. I don't know what it's like to lose a child, but I do know that my parents would do it all again even knowing the outcome. They certainly don't feel that their purpose has been diminished as a result of Doug's death.

And what about those of us who choose not to have children? Is there another purpose for us? When I think about Doug, I can't point to a concrete contribution he made. Does that mean his life didn't matter? Doug was a generous man. He let friends stay with him when they were hard up, bought their kids presents, took in a stray cat, and donated money he scarcely had because others needed it more than him. Generosity may not be something tangible, but does that make it less important?

I pondered this the next morning, July 23, as I settled in at Steamboat. My intent was to sit there until it erupted, which I sincerely hoped would only be a day rather than fifty years. I planned on being alone with my thoughts, but a string of fellow travelers began stopping by. People from all over the country sat next to me and chatted. Some only stayed for a few minutes, and others stayed for hours. We shared our life stories and had some good laughs.

As the day turned into night, the temperature fell and people began to leave. By midnight, Steamboat still hadn't gone off, and only four of us remained. It was dark and cold and the other three remarkably fell asleep. I have trouble sleeping in the best of circumstances, so there was no way I was falling asleep with my teeth chattering, while sitting in an uncomfortable chair in the middle of bear country.

As I shook from the cold and kept my head on a swivel to avoid becoming someone's next meal, I thought about my eulogy. Would it talk about all the geysers I had seen erupt? Would anyone really care if I had seen Steamboat? I concluded that they would not. As my friend brilliantly pointed out, people don't remember the things we do so much as the way we made them feel. The family and friends I leave behind will remember the laughs we shared, the times I helped them out, and the impact I made on their lives.

Whether we live for one year or one hundred, we have the ability to make a lasting impression—both good and bad—on others. We can choose to make a positive impact on those we meet. Even something as simple as a smile and a compliment can brighten their day. Our kindness can change lives.

At 2:30 in the morning, I realized that I may not know what my exact purpose is in this life, but it most certainly isn't to see Steamboat. I quietly gathered my things and began the long trek back to the parking lot in the darkness. I alternated between walking and running, trying to decide which would be least likely to catch the attention of hidden creatures. I made it to my car and drove to the hotel. After a few hours of sleep, I drove roughly ten hours home. Steamboat erupted shortly after I left Yellowstone.

I still haven't seen Steamboat erupt and doubt I ever will. I don't regret the trip because I met some amazing people I'll never forget. Life is, above all, about the connections we make. Losing Doug helped me understand what's truly important in life. We're only here for a limited time, and it's up to us to make the best of it.

Ever since the end of January, I've felt an urge to help others who are going through similar grief. There's so much suffering among suicide loss survivors. In sharing my story, maybe others will realize that they, too, have the strength to make it through to the other side of grief. It isn't easy, but nothing worth doing ever is. I don't want Doug's death to be in vain, so perhaps my story can be our joint contribution to the world.

Letting Go

I have repeatedly referred to grief as a journey, because it's just that. It's not meant to be a destination. I believe I have made it through my grief journey, but that in no way implies that I don't miss my brother or that I've gotten over him. To me, grief is like acute, debilitating pain that is so intense you can focus on nothing else. Even the most menial tasks seem insurmountable. Little things like taking a shower and paying bills feel monumental. Grief is like an ocean, and the waves threaten to sweep us away.

Many suicide loss survivors turn to alcohol in the aftermath. The pain is so deep that it can be appealing to numb it in any way possible. I hadn't had a drink in about nine months prior to Doug's death, but I contemplated it immediately afterward. I didn't want to feel the overwhelming emotions that were overcoming me. But I thought about what Doug would want. Doug had been an alcoholic at one point in his life, and then he stopped cold turkey. I was so proud of him for having the strength to quit. He hadn't touched a drop of alcohol in the years leading up to his death, and I knew he wouldn't want me to turn to alcohol either.

Ultimately, we have to feel all the excruciating emotions at some point. If we don't do so in the immediate aftermath, they will make an appearance when we least expect them. I decided to feel them all as they came. I let myself cry and feel anger. I acknowledged my guilt and regret. I looked at pictures of family vacations, and I read the cards and letters Doug had given me over the years, and I sobbed. I still cry occasionally, nearly a year later, and I'm sure I always will. However, it isn't as frequent, and my tears don't last as long. I'd prefer to deal with the tears as they come, rather than keep them bottled up until I implode.

I'll always be sad over the loss of my brother. That's not to say I don't ever feel happy or joyful. I have fun, and I laugh. The difference is that everything is slightly muted now. The sky is still blue, but it's not quite as bright as it once was. I think about Doug all the time, and I'm very aware that he's no longer physically here. Sadness, unlike grief, is more of a constant ache. It's not debilitating, but it's always present. Some days it downright hurts, and other days my conscious mind barely registers it. But whether or not I'm actively thinking about Doug, melancholy is lurking just below the surface.

I have learned to take it one day at a time. Thinking about spending the rest of my life without Doug is too overwhelming. Breaking it down into more manageable timeframes is essential. It's the difference between observing the entire ocean as a whole and tracking only one wave as it makes its way to the shore. I focus on the present and what I need to accomplish now, rather than looking far into the future.

In order to reach the other side of grief, I had to let go of my guilt and regret. I felt guilt over my last interaction with Doug, as well as the approximately eight months during which we were estranged in 2015 and the hateful things I had said to him surrounding our falling out. I have cried many tears over this and have spent much time despising myself.

Suicide always leaves behind guilt. Because we rarely know exactly why our loved ones took their lives, we assume it had something to do with us. Maybe we did or said something that pushed them over the edge, or maybe it was something we neglected to do or say. Perhaps there was an estrangement, or life was so busy we didn't spend as much time with them as we could have. Once they're gone, we're left unable to apologize or to make up for lost time.

I know that I'm not responsible for my brother's death, just as you're not responsible for your loved one's death. They made their choice and are responsible for their own actions. However, that's of little consolation after they're gone. Seeing a medium helped eliminate my anger toward my brother, but it didn't do much to reduce my guilt and anger toward myself.

Writing out my apology to my brother in letters helped erase some of my guilt, but it didn't eliminate it all. Instead, I started focusing on the positive things I had done during his life that, in my mind, counteracted the negative. For example, Doug and I had a fight over our respective paths in life. Doug called me some derogatory names in reference to my job, and I stormed out the door. I didn't speak to him for several months. Eventually I relented, because I realized it would be too awkward to try and celebrate holidays if we couldn't be in the same room together. And frankly, I missed my brother. I knew if anything happened to him and we hadn't reconciled, I would have trouble forgiving myself. I reached out to him, and he agreed to patch together our fractured relationship. It never fully recovered, but it was better than nothing.

In 2016, I asked Doug to pin my badge during my police academy graduation. It was my second academy, and my dad had pinned my badge on during my first graduation. I was initially going to have my dad do it again, but then I thought it would be nice to ask Doug. I figured he would say no, as he wasn't fond of the police and likely wouldn't want to be in a room full of them. To my surprise, Doug said he would do it. More importantly, Doug sounded quite pleased to have been asked.

On December 1, 2016, I walked across the stage to receive my certificate. I was incredibly nervous that Doug wouldn't be waiting for me on the other side, but there he was with a proud smile. He pinned my badge on my shirt, and we faced the camera with our arms around each other and big smiles on our faces. It can't erase those eight months of not speaking, but when regret and guilt start creeping in, I flash back to that moment on the stage with my brother. In that moment, it was just the two of us again, like old times.

In January 2019, I hired Doug to replace my bathroom floors. It wasn't completely necessary, but Doug had recently replaced the floor in one of his rooms, and I complimented him on how good it looked. He seemed flattered at my praise, which gave me the idea to hire him. Our relationship was still strained, and I thought it would be a nice gesture to pay Doug for some honest work. I would get new floors, and Doug would earn a little extra money. We spent about a week together, and he worked harder than I had ever seen him work before. The finished product looked great, but I was more excited that our bond had strengthened.

We still weren't as close as we had been as kids and young adults, but we were getting there.

When I feel the familiar guilt and regret rear its ugly head, I remember these two moments, among others. Doug knows I loved him and still do. I showed him throughout his life. It's easy to remember the last conversation we had, when I was short with him. That's the interaction that sticks in my mind, but I know it wasn't the one that defined me in his eyes. When a bad memory pops up, try to remember an equally good one to counteract it. I guarantee the good outweighs the bad, for both you and your loved one.

We can't truly heal until we forgive ourselves. Everyone has done or said things we didn't mean and regretted after the fact. That doesn't make us monsters; it makes us human. Depending on the circumstances surrounding the suicide, it may be more difficult to forgive yourself. But blaming yourself for the rest of your life won't accomplish anything. We can't bring our loved ones back, regardless of how much guilt we feel. All we can do is take steps to help us work through the guilt and regret.

Grief is a bit like skydiving. Our loved one's death is akin to leaving the plane. No matter how hard we try, we can't undo what has just happened. We have two choices: do nothing or fight to survive. In the short term, doing nothing is the easier option, but I promise you it won't end well. Fighting takes more energy and strength. It requires us to work hard, and it will be painful at times. But it's the difference between crashing and landing softly. Going to therapy, joining support groups, reading encouraging books, and seeking out mediums are just some of the things we can do to help us survive the freefall. It won't happen overnight, but eventually the waves of grief that once overcame us will become more manageable. They may still rock us, but they will become gentler over time. We will never "get over" the loss of our loved ones, but we can move forward while carrying their memory with us.

Honoring Their Memory

Above all else, our loved ones want us to move on with our lives. They don't want us to be stuck in endless grief. Moving on can be difficult because it feels like we didn't love them enough and are betraying them in some way. We feel guilt every time we smile or laugh. How can we continue to live when they're no longer here? How can life return to normal when a huge part of us is missing?

I have noticed that Doug's signs and visits are much less frequent these days. That devastates me, but I also understand the necessity. Our loved ones don't want us to be so hung up on them that we fail to live our own lives. Signs are frequent in the beginning because they want to make sure we're okay. As time goes on and we begin to heal, they start to pull away. They do this out of love. Their spirits are still with us, but they take on the role of spectator. They may still visit occasionally when we need them the most, but they want us to move on and continue living.

The best thing we can do for ourselves and for our loved ones is to keep their memory alive. That's precisely what I was doing when I bought four pieces of cheesecake on my birthday. Of course we ate the fourth piece ourselves, but I like to think Doug saw that extra piece and appreciated the gesture. Our loved ones want us to move on, but they don't want to be forgotten in the process.

The first time it snowed after Doug's death, I flopped down and made a snow angel. I have no idea what compelled me to do that, and I'm sure any potential witnesses found it strange that a woman in her thirties, without a child in tow, was making snow angels. After making the angel, I laid there looking up at the falling snow, and I told Doug that this was my sign for him so that he knew he wasn't forgotten. Ever since, I've made snow angels in the woods near my house every time it snows. Sometimes the snow is so miniscule that it's more of a dirt angel, but I'll continue this tradition for as long as I'm physically able.

Doug enjoyed growing cactuses in the years before his death, and he gave me one for my birthday in 2019. I wasn't thrilled at the time. I don't have a green thumb and have trouble keeping things alive. My dog's only saving grace is her loud and obnoxious bark if I don't feed her promptly. As I eyed this cactus that couldn't bark for attention, I knew it didn't stand a chance.

After Doug passed away, that cactus became my lifeline to him. It was, I irrationally thought, the only living part of him I had left. I watched as it began turning brown, and I fretted over what to do. Cacti are fairly easy plants that do well with neglect, yet I was somehow managing to kill it. I repotted it in fresh soil, and I started watering it less out of fear that it was rotting. I even contemplated performing surgery to excise the brown areas, and I read cactus forums in an attempt to diagnose and save Doug's cactus. I reluctantly acknowledged that an attempt at surgery would doom the cactus for sure, and I nervously monitored it for any additional changes. It has been about six months since I started noticing the change in colors, and I'm happy to report the cactus is still with us. It doesn't look great, but it's hanging on. And I'm now past the point of associating this specific cactus with Doug. If the cactus dies, I'll simply buy another one. I'll always have a cactus in my home in Doug's memory, but I'll not beat myself up when they die. The cactus isn't Doug; it's merely something we shared and always will.

I had never celebrated Day of the Dead until Doug died. About a week before November 1, 2020, I read about how some cultures celebrate their loved ones who have passed by lighting a candle and baking their favorite foods. I knew right then that I would celebrate by baking gingerbread cookies for Doug, because he had enjoyed them so much when I made them the previous Christmas. Although I had to work, I baked the cookies in advance and, after work that evening, I lit a candle and placed the cookies next to Doug's urn. I spoke to him and told him I loved him. Day of the Dead 2020 was the start of a new tradition, a new way to honor Doug's memory.

My favorite time of the year is the holiday season, and 2020 is no exception. However, my excitement is duller than usual, and I dread the empty chair at the table and the empty spot on the floor where Doug would sit to open his presents. But I'll make sure Doug is part of our festivities nonetheless. I bought two beautiful Christmas ornaments, one for my tree and one for my parents' tree, that say "Forever in our hearts," with Doug's name and years of birth and death. We will still set his spot at the dining room table. It won't be the same, but at least he will still be with us in spirit.

As the years go by, these traditions may change. However, I'll always find a way to carry Doug's memory with me. Although our relationship has changed, our story isn't over. Doug's spirit is still very much here, but he's no longer tethered to the ground. Doug is flying free, and he is at peace.

One of my greatest fears following the death of my only sibling was being asked if I have any siblings. Saying yes invites more questions, which is painful and awkward. Saying no feels terribly wrong, like a denial of the first thirty-four years of my life. So instead I say, "I have a brother in heaven." His body may be gone, but his spirit lives on. He's still a part of my past, present, and future. Doug has always been, and will always be, my big brother.

Author's Biography

Keli Hoffmann lost her only sibling to suicide in 2020, and she has been dedicated to reducing the stigma of suicide and helping other suicide loss survivors ever since. Keli is a deputy sheriff and lives with her dog, Zoey, near Denver, Colorado.

www.ingramcontent.com/pod-product-compliance
Lightning Source LLC
LaVergne TN
LVHW041338080426
835512LV00006B/522